Hey, folks! Thanks for purchasing
this coloring book. You're supporting
an independent artist (that's me!!!).
How very punk rock of you!

While this book was inspired by an iconic film,
all artwork was designed by me.
Please no photocopying, redistributing,
or selling of these pages.

Post your masterpieces on TIKTOK and tag me!
@nya.coloring.book

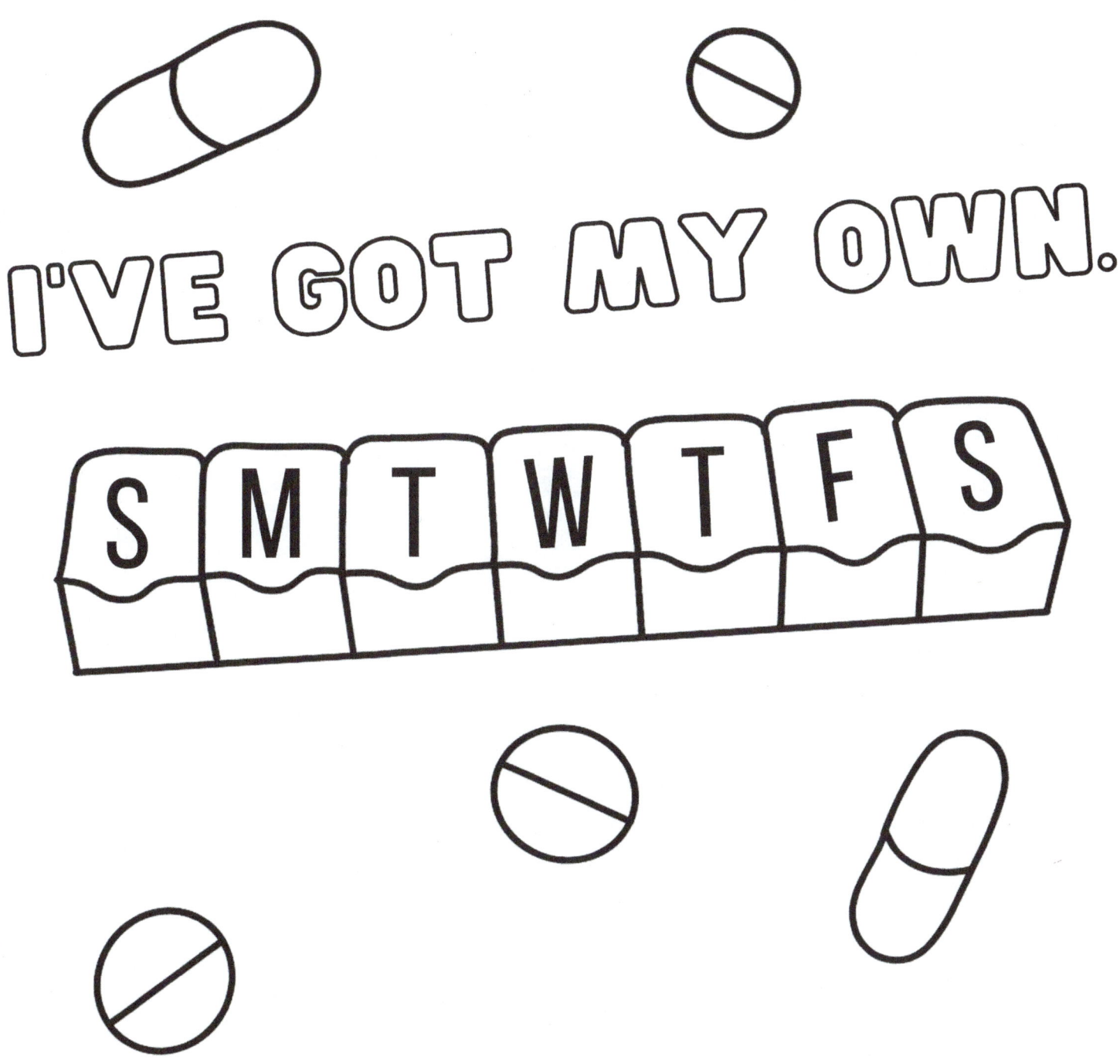

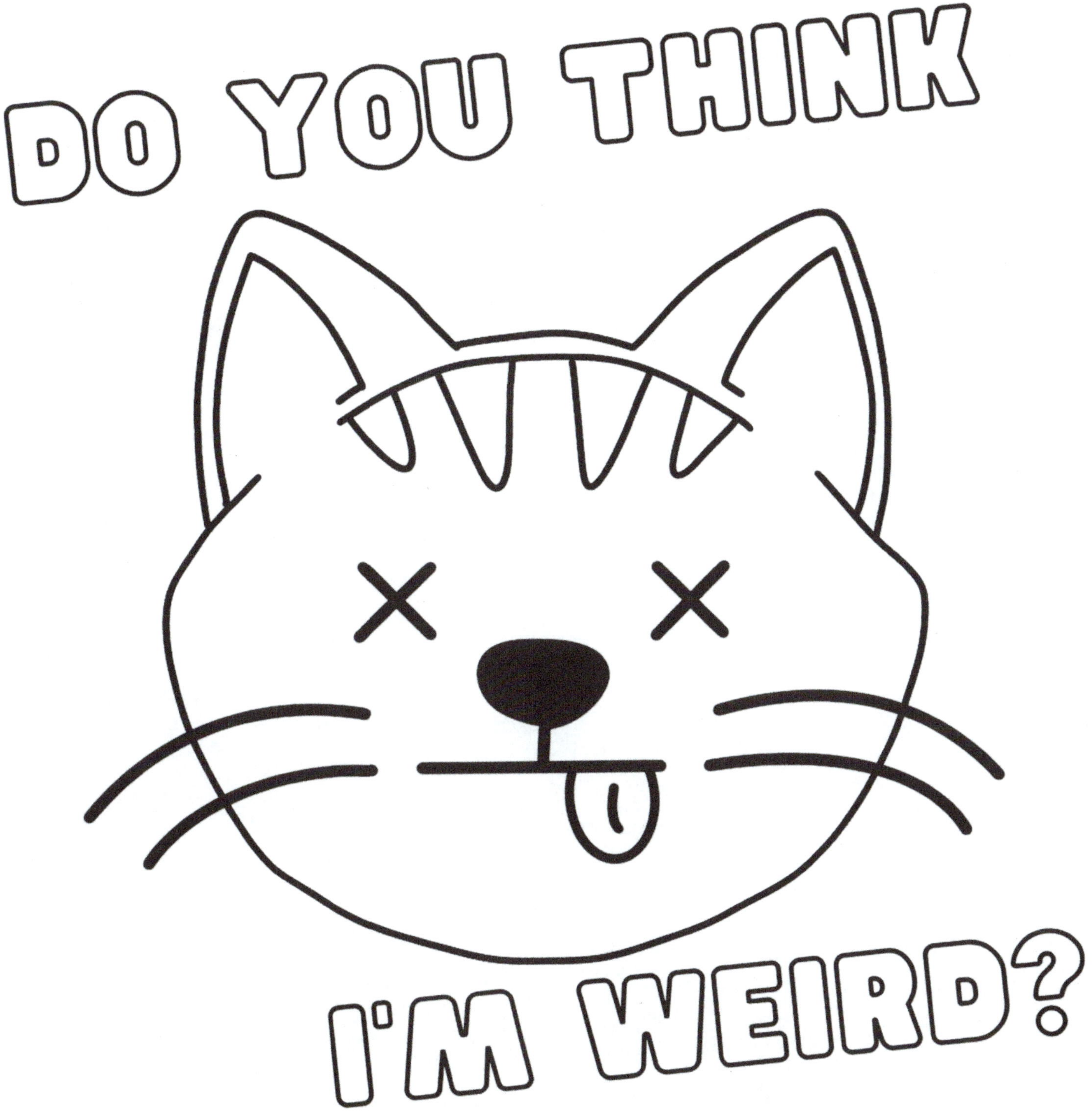
DO YOU THINK
I'M WEIRD?

Made in the USA
Las Vegas, NV
26 January 2025

16911003R00024